A YEAR OF FESTIVALS

Hindu Festivals

Honor Head

Explore the world with Popcorn – your complete first non-fiction library.

Look out for more titles in the Popcorn range. All books have the same format of simple text and striking images. Text is carefully matched to the pictures to help readers to identify and understand key vocabulary. www.waylandbooks.co.uk/popcorn

First published in paperback in 2012
Copyright © Wayland

Wayland
Hachette Children's Books
338 Euston Road
London NW1 3BH

Wayland Australia
Level 17/207 Kent Street
Sydney NSW 2000

 Produced for Wayland by
White-Thomson Publishing Ltd
www.wtpub.co.uk
+44 (0)843 208 7460

Editor: Jean Coppendale
Designer: Paul Cherrill
Craft artwork: Malcolm Couch
Picture researcher: Georgia Amson-Bradshaw
Hinduism consultant: Beryl Dhanjal
Series consultant: Kate Ruttle
Design concept: Paul Cherrill

British Library Cataloging in Publication Data
Honor Head.
    Hindu festivals. -- (A year of festivals)(Popcorn)
    1. Fasts and feasts--Hinduism--Juvenile literature.
    2. Hinduism--Rituals--Juvenile literature.
    I. Title II. Series
    294.5'36-dc22

ISBN: 978 0 7502 6973 5

Wayland is a division of Hachette Children's Books,
an Hachette UK company.
www.hachette.co.uk

Printed and bound in China

Picture Credits: Art Directors: Helene Rogers 16;
Corbis: Raminder Pal Singh/EPA 5; Julian Kumar/
Godong 11; Arko Datta/Reuters 13; Sanjeev Gupta/
EPA 14; Ajay Verma/Reuters 15; Annie Owen/Robert
Harding World Imagery 19; Dreamstime: Ashwin
Kharidehal Abhirama 12; Karsten Koehler 21; 17;
Chris Fairclough: 18/front cover; Photolibrary:
Ephotocorp 4; Christopher Cormack 6; Yogesh S More
7; Photos India 8; Shutterstock: Kailash K Soni 2/9;
Christophe Testi 10; Stephane Breton 1/20

Every effort has been made to clear copyright. Should
there be any inadvertent omission, please apply to the
publisher for rectification.

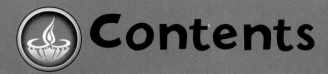# Contents

Colourful Holi	4
The story of Holi	6
Raksha Bandhan	8
Janmashtami	10
Ganesha's birthday	12
Dussehra	14
Durga Puja	16
The Diwali story	18
Diwali and Lakshmi	20
Make a Diwali light	22
Glossary	24
Index	24

Colourful Holi

Holi is a special festival that takes place at the beginning of spring. It celebrates the life of the Hindu god called Krishna.

Krishna is often shown playing the flute.

When Krishna was young he was very playful. One of his favourite games was to throw coloured powder over his friends.

Children dressed as Krishna and his friends throw coloured powder over each other as part of the Holi fun.

Hindus belong to a religion called Hinduism.

The story of Holi

Holi is also about the Hindu story of Holika, an evil witch. The king ordered Holika to kill his son, Prahlad, because Prahlad did not obey him.

At Holi, children put on plays telling the story of Holika and Prahlad.

Holika tried to kill Prahlad by burning him on a bonfire. But Holika lost her magic powers and she was killed on the bonfire instead.

During Holi, people light fires to remember the death of Holika.

Raksha Bandhan

In August, there is a festival for brothers and sisters. It is called Raksha Bandhan. Sisters tie a rakhi bracelet around their brother's wrist.

Rakhi bracelets are made of thread and beads.

Hindus believe a rakhi bracelet will keep the brother safe from harm.

Brothers promise to love their sisters and to look after them. Then the family share some delicious Indian sweets.

Sisters buy or make special sweets to share with their brothers.

Janmashtami

Janmashtami is a festival that celebrates the birthday of the god Krishna. Hindus believe Krishna was born at midnight, so lots of people stay awake all night.

Many people celebrate Krishna's birthday by singing and watching Indian dancing.

Hindus go to the temple to pray. They eat a special food made from milk because this was Krishna's favourite food.

Some temples have statues and pictures of Krishna when he was little.

Janmashtami takes place in August or September.

11

Ganesha's birthday

Ganesha is a Hindu god with an elephant's head. His birthday is celebrated in August or September.

Ganesha is the god of good luck and success.

In the city of Mumbai, in India, there is a special parade on Ganesha's birthday. A big statue of Ganesha is carried through the streets to the sea.

People watch as the statue of Ganesha is carried into the water.

In Mumbai Ganesha's birthday lasts for 11 days.

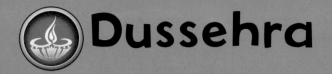 # Dussehra

In September, the festival of Dussehra takes place. This is when people celebrate good winning over bad. Many people act out the story of the god Rama and his fight with wicked Ravana.

This big model of Ravana is made with wood and paper.

Dussehra lasts for ten days. At the end of the festival, burning arrows are fired into the model of Ravana to show that Rama won the fight.

When the model of Ravana is on fire, everyone cheers.

Durga Puja

Durga Puja is a nine-day festival in October. At this time, Hindus remember how the goddess Durga saved the world from a demon that looked like a buffalo.

Durga is a powerful goddess who is often shown riding a tiger.

Many people like to buy new clothes for Durga Puja. They pray at the temple, visit friends and share special meals together.

People gather to watch a play of Durga fighting the demon.

The Diwali story

Diwali is about the story of Rama
and his wife, Sita. They were sent
away from their home to live
in the forest.

During Diwali, Hindus offer food to Rama and Sita.

When Rama and Sita came home, people lit lights to welcome them. At Diwali, Hindus light candles and lamps in their homes and temples.

Special lights, called divas, are made to celebrate Diwali.

Diwali is also called the festival of lights.

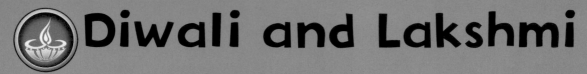 Diwali and Lakshmi

Diwali is also a time when Hindus ask the goddess Lakshmi to come into their homes. They wear their best clothes and give each other cards and presents.

Hindus believe the goddess Lakshmi will bring them happiness and good luck.

Diwali lasts for five days in October and November.

For Diwali, many Hindus make special patterns on the ground outside their front doors. These are called rangoli patterns. They are very bright and colourful.

This rangoli pattern is made from coloured sand.

Make a Diwali light

Join in the festival of lights by making your own paper diva lamp.

You will need:
- Sheet of paper about 30 cm x 21 cm (A4)
- Saucer or plate
- A pair of safety scissors
- Glue stick
- Crayons or felt tips
- Sparkle or sequins to decorate

1. Fold the paper in half from top to bottom.

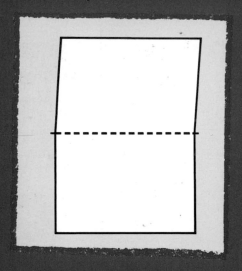

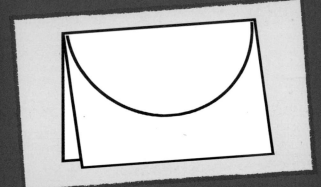

2. Use a saucer or plate to draw a semicircle on one side.

3. Cut out the semicircle. This is the diva.

Colour your diva.

4. Trace this flame outline on to the leftover paper.

5. Colour the flame red then cut it out.

6. Put a little glue at the bottom of the flame and stick it to the middle of the diva.

Add sequins and sparkle to decorate your diva.

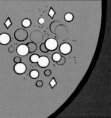

Glossary

buffalo a big cow-like animal that lives in India and other hot countries

demon a wicked being that is not human and who has special powers it uses to scare or hurt people

god a person who is not human with special powers to help people

goddess a woman who is not human with special powers

rangoli a pattern made with coloured sand or powder. It is usually seen outside houses in India on special occasions.

temple a special place where Hindus go to pray

Index

bonfires 7
buffalo 16

dancing 10
demon 16, 17
divas 19
Diwali 18, 19, 20, 21
Durga Puja 16
Dussehra 14, 15

Ganesha 12
god 4, 12, 14
goddess 16, 20

Hinduism 5
Holi 4, 5, 6, 7
Holika 6, 7

Janmashtami 10, 11

Krishna 4, 5, 10, 11

Lakshmi 20

plays 6, 17
Prahlad 6, 7

rakhi bracelet 8
Raksha Bandhan 8
Rama 14, 18
rangoli 21
Ravana 14

Sita 18

sweets 9

temple 11, 17, 19